WINNING SALES

Forthcoming titles in this series will include

- Winning CVs
- Win–Win Negotiation
- Coping with Company Politics
- How to Wow an Audience
- Coping Under Pressure
- How to Pay Less Tax
- Make the Most of Meetings
- Key Account Management

Do you have ideas for subjects which could be included in this exciting and innovative series? Could your company benefit from close involvement with a forthcoming title?

Please contact David Grant Publishing Limited
80 Ridgeway, Pembury, Tunbridge Wells, Kent TN2 4EZ
Tel/Fax +44 (0)1892 822886
Email GRANTPUB@aol.com
with your ideas or suggestions.

This book is to be returned on or before the last date stamped below. £4.99

658.872

SANDY UPPER SCHOOL LIBRARY

60 Minutes Success Skills Series

10778

Copyright © John Frazer-Robinson 2000

First published 2000 by
David Grant Publishing Limited
80 Ridgeway
Pembury
Kent TN2 4EZ
United Kingdom
Tel/fax ++44 (0)1892 822886

03 02 01   10 9 8 7 6 5 4 3 2 1

60 Minutes Success Skills Series is an imprint of
David Grant Publishing Limited

All rights reserved. Except for the quotation of short passages for the
purposes of criticism and review, no part of this publication may be
reproduced, stored in a retrieval system, or transmitted, in any form or by
any means, electronic, mechanical, photocopying, recording or otherwise,
without the prior permission of the publisher.

British Library Cataloguing in Publication Data
A CIP catalogue record for this book is available from the British Library

ISBN 1-901306-35-6

Cover design: Liz Rowe
Text design: Graham Rich
Production coordinator: Paul Stringer
Edited and Typeset in Futura by Kate Williams
Printed and bound in Great Britain by
T.J. International Ltd, Padstow, Cornwall

This book is printed on acid-free paper

The publishers accept no responsibility for any investment or financial decisions
made on the basis of the information in this book. Readers are advised always to
consult a qualified financial adviser.

All names mentioned in the text have been changed to protect the identity of the
business people involved. Any resemblance to existing companies or people is
entirely coincidental.

Contents

Welcome: *About Winning Sales Letters* — 7

Chapter 1: The Best Advice You Can Get — 9
　It's easy when you know how
　Sales letter, mailshot, fax or e-mail?
　The best advice you can get
　Letters are different

Chapter 2: Choose your Formula for Success — 17
　Introducing AIDA
　A creative APPROACH
　The GOLDEN formula
　NOW BUY!
　Bob Stone's 7-step gem

Chapter 3: Rules, Tips and Hints — 33
　The curse of assumption
　How people read letters
　Asking for what you want
　Business or home? What's the difference?
　What's the question?
　The long and the short of it
　Five ways to start a letter

Chapter 4: Looking at Layout — 45
　Shaping up for readership
　Using the keyboard
　Thank you, Mr Johnson
　Using letterheads
　Using design

Chapter 5: What to Say – and Getting it Read — 55
　The pull of a proposition
　Words with power
　When you write
　Adding enclosures

WELCOME

ABOUT *WINNING SALES LETTERS*

Can you really learn enough in just one hour to help you to produce top-class sales letters? The answer is a resounding "Yes". This book provides you with a blueprint that will point you in all the right directions, and gives you lots of tips and techniques to make your letter-writing both professional and successful.

The 60 Minutes Success Skills Series is written for people with neither the time nor the patience to trawl through acres of jargon and management-speak. Like all the books in the series, *Winning Sales Letters* has been written in the belief that you can learn all you really need to know quickly and without hassle. The aim is to distil the essential, practical advice you can use straightaway.

How to get the most from this book

Take a read. Gulp it all down in one go. Then give yourself a little more time to think about how you can best use all the advice and ideas given. The great thing about winning sales letters is you'll find they are well worth your time and thought. Given another read, you'll be able to relate what the book says to your own business, your own desires and intentions, and your own experience. From then on, re-read a chapter a week and go on re-reading at that pace until you feel you've really absorbed it.

But mostly, keep it handy when you are actually writing your sales letters. Dip into it to remind yourself what the book suggests and to stay fresh. Check your progress out against all the checklists, tips, hints and formulae.

> In the JFR's Essential Secrets Series we use highlighted boxes like this to bring particular tips, hints and advice to your attention. In this book I have introduced another kind of box to give you examples. These are not designed to be prescriptive examples. Look at the example and ask yourself 'how should I do that – how could my business use that idea?'

WINNING SALES LETTERS

It is my objective with this book to give you, in about an hour, all you need to know to become a skilled letter-writer. It is unlikely, however, that you can achieve your best letter-writing potential in just one hour. Practice makes perfect, as the saying goes.

Good luck!

THE BEST ADVICE YOU CAN GET — Chapter 1

Coming up in this chapter....

It's easy when you know how
Sales letter, mailshot, fax or e-mail?
The best advice you can get
Letters are different

It's easy when you know how!

Writing winning sales letters is like most other things – it's easy when you know how. In straightforward simple terms this book sets out the principles which will enable you to become a brilliant letter-writer. One of the qualifications I have to write this book is that for 17 years I was the creative director of one of the most respected direct mail companies in Europe. During that time I won more British direct marketing awards for copywriting and creativity than any other individual. But take heart – I'm telling you this not to boast, but to tell you that I had no formal training. I was not even a writer when I started.

You do not need to be a sensational copywriter to write winning sales letters. If you can sell face-to-face, with practice you can do it on paper. If you are not sure of your sales abilities, letters are a perfect way to try them out. It isn't live. You get time to think things through before you do them. And you can change things up to the very last minute.

Yet many people find it daunting when the blank page or screen first appears. That is quite normal. I sometimes still find it daunting myself. If you feel like this, don't worry. It will fade with time and as your confidence builds.

On your bike!

You can think of good letter-writing as like learning to ride a bike. What we'll do is get you up, take those first wobbly steps together, explain a few things and then get some practice.

A frail old lady was wandering along a street in New York. Seeing a smiling cop she approached him and asked, "How do I get to Carnegie Hall?"
"Lady," he said, "you gotta practice!"
From a 1960s TV ad, for I can't remember who.

Sales letter, mailshot, fax or e-mail?

Whether you are writing a one-off sales letter, preparing some standard letters for regular use – or even if you are preparing a direct mail shot – this book will help you. You can use most of the advice on these pages whether your letter is going through the mail, being faxed or e-mailed.

Before we go any further, it is important to note that letters, mailings, faxes and even e-mails can create legally binding commitments between you, your company and the recipient.

The best advice . . .

My secretary, Rosemary, was with me for 14 years, until she ran off with her husband! One day I heard her feet on the stairs outside my office and with her customary tap on the door she opened it and peered round. "Oh!" she said, "you're writing copy. I'll come back." "OK," I responded.

I heard her start back down the stairs, and then it dawned on me. How did she know what I was writing?

"Rooosemarrrry!"

Ever-smiling Rosemary returned to my office and reappeared around the door. "Yes?"

"How did you know I was writing copy?" I asked.

"Simple," she laughed, "you're sitting on the opposite side of your desk. You always do when you're writing copy. I always assumed you were sort of putting yourself in the place of the reader."

In all those years I'd never consciously noticed what I was doing.

The best thing you can do with a formula

The method we are going to use is simple. I shall give you some formulae to look at. And then, after some basic rules, tips and hints, you'll be ready to start writing winning sales letters. You'll find that, as your confidence grows, you'll begin to work without the formulae. The tips and hints are embedded in your mind and you're away. But, most important, like riding a bike, you'll have developed a skill which you can bring out and use whenever you need it. You'll also find that all your other letters and documents will improve in quality and become more effective too.

You might find it surprising that there are several formulae in this book since I don't really believe in writing letters – or any copy for that matter – to a formula. In fact I believe that when it comes to writing copy, the best thing you can do with a formula is throw it away. However, the second best thing to do with a formula is to follow it slavishly! Let me explain.

When you write to a formula, the copy tends to be lumpy and awkward. It's as if the writer has treated the formula as a checklist and is ticking things off as they go along. "I've done that, now what do I have to do next?" The result is copy that doesn't flow. It's like one module follows along after another. However, once the formula is embedded into your thinking and you follow its process naturally, then you write good copy which flows, is easy to read, and has a compelling rationale to it. It also interests the reader and convinces them that they should take the action, buy or enquire. It's compelling.

The best way to use a formula

I do believe in using a formula to evaluate or assess the effectiveness of copy. This can be useful when you have written something yourself or are asked an opinion by a colleague or even when you have paid for a professional to write a letter for you. If you should be fortunate enough to give your letter-writing to someone else, an advertising copywriter for example, you will need to remember that there are some differences between sales letters and other documents such as leaflets and brochures. Letters are generally less formal, conversational and not written in the third person, for example. You will probably come to your own realisation of the distinguishing features of letter-writing as you read on through the book.

If you are looking for professional help, be sure you get someone who understands how the craft of letter-writing differs from other advertising copywriting or scriptwriting.

> **Lesley wanted to be a writer. Her grammar was useless and her spelling appalling. She was quite open about that at her interview. However she had a degree in psychology, good experience of selling and, I don't know ... something about her convinced me she could make it as a writer. I took her on.**
>
> **"Well," said Lesley as we were sitting together at the close of her first day, "you are considered the master of this art that I have to learn. What's the best advice you can give me, a pearl of wisdom to set me off down your path, the secret of your success?"**
>
> **I didn't have one. "Give me 'til morning, Lesley, I'll give it some thought." I wrangled all evening with what to tell her but next day presented her with a card which said:**
>
> > Write what the reader wants to read,
> > NOT what the writer wants to write.
>
> **I believe this to be the best piece of advice I have ever given on this topic and have given it many times since. Try it. It is not always easy, but it is always effective.**

The first thing to consider

The first thing you ought to consider is whether a letter is the most appropriate way to communicate the information or proposition you have in mind. That might sound strange but many times I have sat with groups of people during my master classes and reflected with them on the advice I gave Lesley. For example, suppose you want to announce a price increase. Most groups immediately come to the conclusion that they would want to deal with some Customers differently to others. With major Customers, sales people often prefer to handle the announcement during a visit rather than by letter. If a letter is the best option, will you post it, e-mail it or fax it?

Letters are different

So what exactly makes letter copy different from copy for leaflets or flyers or press ads? Most other copy is written in the third person. Letters are from me to you. They can be more personal. "Write as you speak" is my advice. Letters come from people: leaflets come from companies. Letters bring news or explain things. Letters are sent by individuals; they have a signature at the bottom to prove it. Letters can be more friendly and, in the right situations, even chatty. Good letters, mass produced or a one-off, can – indeed, should – relate to the reader, their life and situation.

Letters can have a pleasant, almost disarming lack of formality, without being pretentious, precocious or presumptuous. They are also polite. They wait until you are ready for them. They don't shout over you like the radio or television. They 'talk' – yes, that's the word – for they are usually very conversational in a pleasant easy sort of way. Most are lively and fun to read. Some stimulating. Some moving. Some newsworthy. Some quite valuable. Letters can even tell stories.

And letters are intimate – they are yours. They come to you, often with your name on. And you read them to yourself. And if you decide to share your letter with someone else then you can, which is unusual for a sales message. Some of it has to do with the fact that they are undoubtedly the only sales copy that starts "Dear" and ends "Yours": a final pledge of faith, sincerity or truth.

Take it from the top

A letter should have a beginning, a middle and an end. The beginning is used to gain interest and put across the strongest point you want to make or the biggest benefit you have to offer. The middle is where you expand and explain and the end is where you summarise with a call to action. Don't vary from the rationale. Stay to the point. Don't bury great stuff in the main body and lead off or make headlines and sub-heads from relative trivia. Concentrate on this point because I see people failing at it all the time – even professionals who should know better.

WINNING SALES LETTERS

The opening is all important

You will lose more readers in the first 50 words than you will in the next 250. Openings are incredibly important – make good use of them! It often pays to invest a few words building up interest and readership, but don't do it at the expense of the most important benefit to the reader. Why not use the main benefit to build your readers' excitement and anticipation?

Letters need to be stimulating and interesting and relevant to the reader – and when they are being sent to someone with whom you have already had contact, they should make reference to the state of the relationship between you and your business and the recipient and their business

> **Use the information you have on record to make your letter relevant to the reader.**
>
> Dear Mr Wilson,
>
> Five New Pacific Models are waiting for you to test drive them.
>
> It was good to see you last month when you brought your wife's car in for service. We certainly appreciate your continued custom. Since you were last here there has been a great deal of excitement with the arrival of five new models in the Pacific range. Indeed, as you are a regular and valued Customer here at Stone & Co, I'd like you to be among the very first to take them for a spin and discover all the advanced new features and options available . . .

Writing sales letters is very like any other form of selling. You need to be confident, have good self-esteem and be motivated. Once you have got them reading they will only quit if you:

- ○ stop being interesting
- ○ say something they dislike or disagree with
- ○ fail to hold them
- ○ confuse them or become too much like hard work
- ○ are not good fun, pleasant or good company to be with.

> Before you start writing organise your thoughts and brief yourself. List the points you want to make and then prioritise them from the reader's point of view.

THE BEST ADVICE YOU CAN GET

Ask for action!

Close your letter asking for the action you want. Never worry about repetition as long as you are still being interesting.
A PS after the signature is a strong device, but be warned that it rarely gets read last – it is often read after the headline and before the main text.

1. It's easy when you know how – you do not have to be a trained or professional writer to write winning sales letters.
2. Use a formula to get the process and structure of sales letters into your head – with practice the result becomes naturally flowing copy.
3. Always try to "write what the reader wants to read, not what the writer wants to write".
4. Be sure that a letter is the most appropriate way of communicating the message and also consider the actual delivery mechanism before you start writing.
5. Whether a one-off letter, a form letter or a mailing, whether transmitted by post, fax or e-mail, a letter is a legally binding document between you, your company and the recipient.
6. Letter-writing is different to other forms of copywriting. Letters are best written in the first person not the third person and they can be less formal, more personal and should, as best as possible, relate to the reader as an individual – even in mailings.
7. You lose more readers in the first 50 words than you will in the next 250. Openings are incredibly important! Make good use of them.
8. Remember these basic principles:
   - letters have a beginning, a middle and an end
   - start with your biggest benefit, expand and summarise with a call to action
   - letters being sent to someone with whom you already have contact or a relationship should refer to that situation and be personalised
   - don't worry about repetition – but change the way you say things
   - many letters will benefit from a strong PS.

CHOOSE YOUR FORMULA FOR SUCCESS — Chapter 2

Coming up in this chapter

Introducing AIDA
A creative APPROACH
The GOLDEN formula
NOW BUY!
Bob Stone's 7-step gem

Working with a formula

This chapter contains a number of different ideas for you to try. Read through it. Decide which of them you like best or which best suits the next letter-writing project you have. Then make a start. If you have trouble deciding on your opening use one of the five ideas in Chapter 3. After you've had a go and your letter is complete, pick another formula to assess your copy.

> For assessment of copy, I have always found AIDA the most effective. It is simple and sweet and follows a natural, human process.

Introducing AIDA

AIDA stands for Attention, Interest, Desire, Action. Grab the reader's attention, stimulate interest, build desire – to do whatever it is you are writing to them about – and then call for action. It is a simple, magic formula. And it works every time. Its simplicity makes it ideal for beginners. However, although simple, it lacks sophistication. This is probably one to start you off, but move on to one of the others after a while. However, once a letter is written, AIDA is always a stunning, quick and easy copy appraisal tool for reviewing letters.

Getting started

With at least half the letters that people show me, one simple improvement can be made right away by chopping out the first paragraph. We seem to love waffling starts! This is what I call the "crescendo". It works well in music but badly in letter-writing. A second type of crescendo is where the poor reader has to endure about five paragraphs before the main event is actually mentioned. The writer feels the need to explain things first and then come up with the real reason for writing.

Start with the most interesting topic, the biggest benefit, the most important thing from the reader's point of view. Grab them straight away, get them into the body of your letter and then they are more likely to stay with you. Never crescendo!

Now let's take a creative APPROACH

APPROACH is an acronym for Arrive, Propose, Persuade, Reassure, Organise an opportunity, Ask for the order (or response), Clarify, Help.

Arrive

What steps have you taken to make the right impression – not just of your letter, but of your company, and what you have to say? Do you look important and interesting enough to merit the investment of the reader's time, energy and attention? If you are creating a mailing or a letter which is going to be used regularly, you should appreciate that for many people at home or working in smaller businesses the letter – or rather the effect you have on the reader – starts actually with the envelope.

Propose

Let them know right away what's in it for them. There is no single bigger turn on for the reader than for them to find the answer to the question "What's in it for me?", which they will all ask immediately. Come out with a strong, credible and desirable answer. Above all be sure to make a strong proposition. More on propositions in Chapter 5.

> **Just three kinds of reader**
>
> There are only three kinds of reader in the whole world.
>   First, there's the YES reader. This reader LOVES you. They love your company. They trust your brand. They buy from you all the time. And whatever it is you are trying to sell today, they'll buy! Sadly, this is an all too rare breed, but they're out there. What do you have to write to sell to them? Answer – nothing! They'll buy because you wrote to them again.
>   Then there's the NO reader. They HATE you. They hate getting sales letters. They hate your company. Yours is the last brand they'd trust. They wouldn't dream of doing business with you if you were the last person left on earth. What do you have to write to sell to them? Answer – nothing! They're hopeless cases and you're wasting your time, effort and money.
>   Then there's the MAYBE reader. They're not sure. They don't mind getting interesting letters even if they are trying to sell something. They may or may not have heard of you but they have an open mind. These are the people you should be writing for as well as to.
>   The problem is, of course, you usually don't know which category the reader is that you are writing to. So write as if you were writing to a MAYBE and you will have the best chance of success.

Persuade

Now set about a confirming process for those in YES gear and a convincing process for those in MAYBE or neutral gear. Prioritise your benefits with the best first and set them out one by one. Cover them all, and have the courage of your convictions. It has cost you time and money to get in front of the reader, so put your mouth (or words) where your money is. Remember, benefits never bore. Benefits never put people off. Just as long as they are real, believable, desirable . . . and, at the end of the day, you can deliver.

Reassure

If you were in the reader's situation what would worry you? Small print? The thought of a medical? Whether you could afford the product or service? Whether a salesperson will call? If the product is new — does it really work, will you get maintenance problems, teething troubles? If it is old, how soon will it be replaced with the new model? If it is far away, like a distant holiday, who'll look after you, handle languages, etc.? If it is complicated, is it worth the trouble and paperwork?

Whatever the potential worries, as the writer, you must address them, reassure your reader that you understand, you have the answers and that they won't be intimidated, embarrassed, regretful or let down. Guarantees are very reassuring.

Orchestrate an opportune opportunity

To persuade people to act or respond, you must give them reasons. One reason should be your proposition. But it is better to convince people to act sooner rather than later — and preferably right away. This is the moment to orchestrate an opportunity for them — in other words, to add an extra level to your proposition which makes the whole concept a good one, but even better if taken now.

There are many ways of devising special offers for these situations and for all levels of society, whether consumer, professional or business-to-business. We all hate to lose out, and we all like to win. Here your task is to lubricate these desires.

> An opportunity is by definition "especially favourable". The direct marketer's favourites here are the bonus offer, the time-close, and the limited edition. They are very powerful but all too easily dismissed as "mail order techniques". You'll find they work brilliantly in many sales letters too.

Ask for the order (or response)

Talk about response as if you expect it, not as if it will surprise you! It's a small point, but the number of times I see this:

CHOOSE YOUR FORMULA FOR SUCCESS

"If you return the reply paid card enclosed . . ."

The very use of the word 'if' unravels almost everything you've done so far. It suggests there is a course other than response. It suggests you believe they might not want to accept your proposition. It suggests that really it might not be all that it's cracked up to be. Have you been lying ? What does this say:

"When you return the enclosed reply paid card . . ."?

It's an entirely different set of implications – more confident, more positive.

Let's make a date

Closing or cut-off dates* are usually good for response. Create a need for one that is genuine: it could be because of a special offer or terms or because you are using incentives where supplies might be limited.

> In deciding how long your closing date should be, think about the decision-making process. A closing date of two weeks on a kitchen, for example, would be very short. The decision cycle there, I am told, can be up to 18 months. In that case, take the process and divide it into bite-size chunks. Narrow the offer down to a particular stage in the process such as a showroom visit and then relate the offer to that stage. A perfect offer would be a free design job when you visit in the next four weeks. The next chunk is probably the "how do we afford it?" stage, so a finance offer would work well. This should continue until the purchase sale is made.

It is often wise with any non-standard offer to specify the duration of availability. Think about the timing carefully. If it is too short it loses business. Not everybody wants to reply to suit your schedule and you must respect that. If it is too long it won't have

---

* If you are dealing with a financial service take heed of the Financial Services Act 1986, which prohibits artificial closing dates.

twenty-one

the desired "hurry up" effect. Indeed, people may actually delay responding because you've told them you'll give them 12 weeks to do it. Once they've put you to one side, whatever their intentions at the time, the likelihood of a positive response is slashed to about a tenth.

Generally between two and four weeks is the best timing. In a sales letter, only give readers more than four weeks if you have a very good reason.

> What has become known as the "early bird" is one answer to this problem and usefully leaves the door ajar for those who want to reply in their own good time. An "early bird" is an extra offer for acting within the timeframe. Make it abundantly clear that it's the extra offer that closes on the chosen date – the proposition is acceptable any time. Another version is to limit the offer to a specific number – say the first 100 to reply.

Clarify

There are two things to clarify. You need to be absolutely certain that you have made your proposition, offer and terms clear to the reader. The best way to do this is to run through it in its entirety again. Don't worry about repeating yourself. That is a good thing as long as you keep it interesting. Use different words to do it.

> **Same thing, different words**
>
> "For just £99" becomes "and remember, it's all for less than £100!" and if you have to say it again later "and you still get change from £100!"

You will also need to be certain that the response methods and procedures are clear to the reader. The blatant way to do this is the most successful way. That's why you see this subhead so often:

"How to apply"

CHOOSE YOUR FORMULA FOR SUCCESS

> This is easy to convert to other forms of words for different uses:
>
> "Please complete and return the enclosed application promptly. You'll find a reply envelope enclosed and no stamp or addressing is needed. Please also be sure to sign and date the . . ."

A stamped addressed envelope is ideal for a one-off or a small number of letters and it emphasises and demonstrates just how much you look forward to a reply.

As you draw to the close of your letter it's quite possible to find ways of weaving the last three pieces of advice together: organising on opportune opportunity, asking for the order and clarifying why and how they should respond.

Help

The more you can do to help the reader, the better. This extends from helping them to afford your product or service (think about easy payment terms and accepting credit cards), to helping them get answers to questions (a telephone hotline or personal extension number?) or just helping them to respond by providing the wherewithal, advice and convenience.

The GOLDEN formula

The acronym this time is GOLDEN. It stands for Grab attention, Open strongly, Lead logically, Demand action, Encourage response, Need it now.

Grab attention

What can you do to grab attention – and hold it? You may want to do this at the beginning of a letter, or earlier, say on the outside of the envelope.

> A long-time supplier wanted to grab my attention to his mailing. On the envelope, otherwise blank apart from the address, he had written a personalised message in block capitals. Mine said simply "GREAT NEWS INSIDE, JOHN!". What a brilliant idea!

Open strongly

The biggest possible benefit to the reader is usually the strongest opening at your disposal. If you are writing a letter for a mailing, you should consider varying this from one recipient to another.

> Vary the opening from one recipient to another. A letter going to a sales director starts:
>
>> "Let me tell you about a product so reliable it virtually sells itself . . ."
>
> To the finance director it starts:
>
>> "Let me tell you about a product that brings extraordinary value at a price that can't be beaten . . ."

Lead logically

A sound sales case generally has a preferred rationale to it. Find it and follow it.

If you are sending more than a letter, try to make sure that all the contents of your envelope follow the same sales rationale. This is one of the main pitfalls of simply strapping on a letter and reply card to a general product leaflet and making do with it as a mailing. If you look at 95 per cent of these sort of mailings the letter and the leaflet present different product or service sales rationales in different sequences. One has to be right. Or at least better! The different rationales may be in harmony, but what you need is unison. Whether you are writing to one person, or ten thousand and one.

CHOOSE YOUR FORMULA FOR SUCCESS

> A sales letter from a potential supplier was recently sent to me. The leaflet, I imagine the work of an ad agency, proclaimed "Quality that leads the world". The accompanying letter started "This letter offers you the lowest prices in Britain!"
>
> One of those claims has to better – and anyway surely the letter can be adopted to bring the two together: "Breathtaking – but true. Quality that leads the world at the lowest prices in Britain. If you are looking for value when you . . ."

Demand action

There is just no getting away from it, the need to demand action from the reader, to spell out what you want, to make it attractive, desirable and urgent, crops up in nearly every worthwhile formula, checklist and, for that matter, book! Closing on a call to action to an attractive and desirable proposition is an absolute must.

> **Go for immediate action**
>
> "Please call me now. I have limited machines available for the 7 DAY FREE TRIAL OFFER and it has to be first come first served . . ."

Encourage response

There are so many ways to nudge, push, prompt, cajole, tease or urge a reply: a gift or incentive, a special offer, discount or saving. And, on top of that, you will encourage more to reply by making the physical act of replying simple in every way. Do they respond by mail or e-mail? Maybe the phone or fax? Or a local branch or outlet? Will you take a credit card payment? All of these can only happen if you provide the information.

> When you are considering the media through which you will encourage response, forget which one is best for you. Organise your response handling to what is best for the responder. If you are writing to a computer person, e-mail

> or a website may be preferable to phone, fax or reply card. Give as many options as you can but never leave out a reply paid card or envelope.

Need it now

That's the level of excitement, enthusiasm and desire you've got to aim for. You've got to make them read about your proposition and think "I need it now". Can you use a time-close? Will you make something extra or a bonus available if they act within the time limit? Or, in a mailing, first come, first served.

> If you've got somebody to say "I need it now", pay them the courtesy of a prompt efficient delivery or response to their action. Otherwise all the hard work you've done will drive them elsewhere to satisfy the need. They will go to your competitors. Or other sources.

NOW BUY!

Our final acronym-style formula is "NOW BUY!" The letters stand for Noticed, Opened, Wanted, Believed, Understood, Yes'd.

Noticed

Will you get noticed when your letter arrives on the mat? Or, if you think your envelope might not be seen, how can you get yourself to stand out or be placed on the top of the pile? Why not try to win in both situations? If you are writing to a business, the rank or status of the individual recipient will make a difference. The proprietor of a very small business probably opens their own mail and therefore sees the envelope. The managing director of a massive business probably doesn't. Yet the vast majority of direct mail going to all sizes of businesses is sent in envelopes with printed messages. Why? Because sufficient get through to make enough difference for it to pay off most of the time. But suppose yours doesn't. How can you get the attention of the reader when you're in a pile of morning mail? Be creative on the envelope!

> With one small mailing I used window envelopes to gain attention. But we addressed the outside of the envelope and used the window intriguingly to show the middle of a bank note. The bank note was an out-of-date Venezuelan Bolivar which had not been in use for some years. It cost next to nothing from a dealer and it was certainly noticed!

Opened

Once noticed, what have you done to ensure that you will be opened? And then what single thing will attract or impress above all else at the opening moment? The figure is lower in Europe, but last year 51 per cent of all direct mail in the USA was thrown away unopened and unread. I wonder why! However wonderful your letter – and even if it is a one-off, not a mailing – all that mail that arrives with your winning sales letter is competing for the same reader's attention and time and possibly money. You have to make an impact and stand out.

> Lots of sales letters go out in response to enquiries. With businesses it pays to differentiate what you send so that a mailroom or secretary doesn't mistake it for an unsolicited mailing. Buy a rubber stamp saying "Here is the information you requested". If you get lots of enquiries, print the envelopes or print some labels.
>
> **Be warned!**
> Don't be tempted to abuse that and use this idea inappropriately. I know someone who did and got hundreds of angry letters and phone calls – not exactly the response he wanted. He just made people feel tricked. Not good for sales! The same advice applies to "Personal" and "Private and Confidential". Abuse them at your peril!

Wanted

You need to approach "wanted" in two ways. First, what can you do to make your letter(s) wanted? If they want to read, there's much more chance they'll want to respond. Second, have you done everything in your power to make the product or service wanted? Have you sold it with flair, enthusiasm and passion? Have you sold it thoroughly? Follow the advice coming up in "Bob Stone's gem" regarding benefits and features depending on whether you are trying to make a sale or get an enquiry.

Believed

Avoid the incredible. Back up your sales story with undeniable fact. In place of opinion and rhetoric, give evidence. Testimonials and case histories serve as good examples.

> **Incredible! And it was**
>
> I once created mailings to generate enquiries for a system of supermarket and other retail display shelving. We mailed many different sectors of retailing. Each sector's mailing contained a winning sales letter (naturally!) together with a real case history featuring the stories of retailers in that sector for whom the shelving had provided increased sales because of the improved displays and merchandising.
>
> The levels of sales increase described in the mailings varied from, a high, in one case, of almost 70 per cent down to 25 per cent. We found that the more modest levels pulled far better response rates. Research revealed that retailers were suspicious of the higher figures – either they felt they were exaggerated or that the result was a one-off and the same thing wouldn't happen for them. The modest results were believed.

Understood

You, and your proposition, must be understood. What you want the reader to do must also be understood. Use clear, simple, jargon-free conversational language and clean, crisp easy-to-follow layouts that make your message easy to absorb.

CHOOSE YOUR FORMULA FOR SUCCESS

> I was reading some copy recently which had been prepared by a large well known agency for a major consultancy Client of mine. The letter was going to be sent to SOHOs – small office, home office businesses. The brief from the Client had pointed out that most people in this group are over 45. Reading the letter you could tell that the writer was about 25 years old, had never worked from home and was completely ignorant about working in or even running a small business. Letters must relate to their readers and build rapport with them. If you don't know anything about the person or people you are writing to – find out!

Yes'd

What have you given people to say "yes" to? Have you phrased your proposition so that "yes" is the obvious, attractive and desirable thing to do? If you have, you've yes'd them!

> **Give them something to say "yes" to**
>
> "Wouldn't you be proud to own the very latest model? Especially if you could tell your family and friends how you took advantage of this incredible offer. Remember, there's nothing to pay for the first three months. Pick up the phone now and it's yours!"

Bob Stone's gem

This final formula comes from US direct marketing expert Bob Stone. It is a gem. Whenever I got blocked or stuck, this one solved the problem for me. I thoroughly recommend this seven-step process.

1. Put the main benefit first

If you are simply writing a one-off sales letter, this shouldn't be a problem as you should be writing what the reader wants to read and therefore focusing on the main benefit from their point of view. If you're letter-writing for a mailing it is possible that the main benefit could be the same for all – for example if you are featuring a fabulous discount. However, in other cases it will pay you to break the audience down into groups of similar people or businesses. Then you can vary the copy to suit the various main benefits for each distinct group.

2. Enlarge on the main benefit, and bring in the secondary benefits

Stay with the main benefit even if you are repeating yourself but use different words – then start explaining all the other benefits. Don't worry about length of copy. It is a complete fallacy that people will not read long letters or more than one page. As long as you are interesting and you are including plenty of reasons to read they will stay with you.

> **The length of the letter should be determined by what you have to say and how interesting you can be about it. Short message, short letter. Longer message, longer letter. It's a bit like how long your legs need to be – long enough to reach the floor! A letter should be long enough to do the job effectively.**

3. Tell the reader precisely what they will get

This stage needs some explanation. Telling the reader precisely what they will get is particularly good advice if you are trying to sell something by mail order. It is important that your reader gets the full picture – all the benefits and all the features. However, where you are trying to stimulate an enquiry, an appointment or store traffic, it can work against you. Stick to the benefits only. Once you get embroiled in the features you are taking away the reader's need to come back to you or visit you for more information. There is nothing left they need to know. And should a sales visit follow, what has the rep got to tell them? The leaflet and letter have already told the prospect everything there is to tell.

CHOOSE YOUR FORMULA FOR SUCCESS

> One delegate attending a workshop told me how they put a product leaflet in all the letters they sent out in response to their press advertising. The conversion rate to appointment was awful. This was because the leaflet included all the benefits and all the features. Why did the recipient need to see their rep? They had everything they could possibly need to know. The company re-designed the leaflet to take out the technical specification and just concentrate on the benefits and offered a free demonstration in the letter. The combined result was, to use their word, "amazing".

4. Back up your story with case histories and endorsements

Remember to keep them credible. Seek the permission of those you wish to quote and, if appropriate, photographs bring the human touch too (yes, even in a letter!)

5. Tell your reader what they might lose if they don't act

This works a treat – and so few people use it! Yet, think of how we all react at the thought of losing a benefit or offer or not being able to get something – last orders in a pub!

> **Tell people what they might lose if they don't act**
>
> "Don't forget! To claim all that FREE PAPER, you must reply in the next fourteen days otherwise you'll miss the boat and your chance is gone forever!"

6. Sum-up by re-stating the benefits, but in a different way

Find a different set of words to summarise your core proposition and the main and secondary benefits again. Be especially sure, since you are repeating things, that you stay interesting.

There's an old expression in selling – "tell them what you are going to tell them, then tell them and then tell them what you told them" – it works just as well in letter-writing.

"What else can you get to match for less than £200? Nothing! At just £195 it is remarkable. I saw a lower specification product at an exhibition last week on special offer at £325. Now here I am writing to you proposing you buy for £130 less than that! But please act quickly . . ."

7. Incite immediate action

You have to do something to make sure you don't get filed or stuck behind the clock on the mantelpiece or in a drawer. As soon as that happens, you've disappeared never to be seen again. Give people a reason to pick up the phone, fax you, whatever. Urge them to do it NOW. If you want an example, read again the last three words of the previous one!

In this chapter we have looked at the best learning process to help you become a writer of winning sales letters and a number of formula-driven solutions for letter-writing.

1. Never crescendo – always start with the main event!
2. There are only three kinds of reader: yes, no and maybe. Write to the maybe reader.
3. Special offers enhance your proposition. Give them a closing date to encourage early response
4. Letters start with the outer envelope – can you use this to your advantage?
5. Case histories and testimonials can add valuable evidence to your sales story – keep them credible

RULES, TIPS AND HINTS — Chapter 3

Coming up in this chapter

The curse of assumption
How people read letters
Asking for what you want
Business or home? What's the difference?
What's the question?
The long and the short of it
Five ways to start a letter

The curse of assumption

There are three assumptions that people make when they write letters – and they are dangerous! So avoid them.

First, don't assume that your letter will be read. As I have said before, you have to make it attractive to read, interesting to read and easy to read. You have to use your letter to earn people's time and attention.

Second, don't assume people will read all your letter. People will skip read. People will lose interest. People will have babies falling out of high chairs, meetings to go to, or a knock at the door. I've no doubt you can recall putting a letter down half way through to answer an incoming call. When you sit and write, as opposed to read, if you're typical, you'll try to do it somewhere and some time when you can get some peace and concentrate. You'll sit and ponder and muse things. Readers do not have that luxury. They don't sit there waiting for your letter, pounce on it when it arrives and then give it their undivided attention.

By using layout, headlines and sub-headlines you can simultaneously give shape and interest to your letter, provide visual and verbal "signposts" for the reader and give them "now where was I?" anchors to help them navigate. When a reader puts your letter down these anchors are the most likely places where they will re-start – think of them like lay-bys at the side of a road. Readers will rarely start from the beginning again.

Third, don't assume they will read the letter in order!

How people read letters

Most written advertising – sales letters or otherwise – is tackled by its reader in three distinct phases. They are the GLANCE, the SCAN, and the READ.

You need to recognise that you must achieve success not once, not twice, but three times as your readers go through the three stages of reading. You must succeed as they glance at it – to get them to move on. You must succeed when they scan it – to get them to move on. And you must succeed when they read it – to get them to absorb, accept and act.

The number of readers will decrease at each stage. But you have to make sure that, as the numbers dwindle, your effort increases on those who remain.

At a glance

The early glancing process is a horrendously fast event. The eye rests on a number of points for just two-tenths of a second. The tolerance level per A4 spread is about ten eye-resting points. Your letter lives or dies in just two seconds! With an A3 spread the tolerance level goes up to about 15 eye-resting points, so you've got three seconds. Then, with the speed of light, the glancer's brain makes a decision. Go again or quit?

Next they scan – then they read

The second trip round – the scan – gives you more time. The scan is all about gathering evidence to justify a read. The glance was picking up odd words and maybe a full phrase but not much else other than feeding the visual sense. Here you'll get whole headlines, photo-captions, and subheads read.

How you fare from here is down to you. With some you'll get the in-depth read. Some will still not decide without a preliminary fast read. Then and only then will they go for the diagrams and more complicated pictures and illustrations then, finally, the body copy.

RULES, TIPS AND HINTS

> **Go with the flow**
>
> Natural eye directions should be built on, not contradicted. With an A4 sheet a reader will want to enter at the top left and leave at the bottom right. With an A3 spread they will enter top right and exit bottom right. Therefore, you have to pull people to the left-hand page using powerful eye-catchers such as photographs. A well-placed photo of a human being is always more powerful than a photo of a product or building.

Think of the "glance, scan, read" method when writing and this will give your letters structure and power – the power of persuasion. Always have a headline, even if it is a simple, centred sentence highlighted with an underline or in bold face. Make sure it has the major benefit included. Then make sure that your subheads tell a short-form version of the story and lead your reader logically through the proposition.

The heaviest readership zones of letters are:

- the recipient's name and address block (we like to check you got it right . . . and woe betide you if you didn't!)
- your name and address
- the signature (large, open and legible)
- the name and title of the signatory
- the PS and the headline.

These are all eye-catchers. You can create more eye-catchers using indented paragraphs, underlining, capitals, bold, and some of the other devices used for emphasis.

> *" I tested exactly the same letter with four different headlines. One of the headlines pulled almost double the response of the worst one! And to think, until recently I never even used them. "*
> **– John Friend, Marketing Manager, Moores by Mail**

When to use a PS

In general a post script is a good thing – it gets high levels of readership and is often read before the main body of the letter. I would include one normally unless you particularly want to look

thirty-five

like a 'regular' letter and keep a conservative or traditional look. A neat idea is to refer to something good that's in the letter. If the reader gets to the PS after they have read the main text then you have got in another reminder. If, as is most often the case, they are one of those who go to it first, you have given them another reason to read – they know there is something waiting for them in the letter!

One way to use a PS so that it works for both a reader who is reading it before the main body of the letter and one who is reading it last is to say "Remember the special offer in the letter is yours to claim whenever you . . .". This way it flags that there is an offer to read about for the former and makes sense to the latter as a reminder.

Ending a page

If you are using more than one page NEVER end the page with a complete sentence or paragraph – except for the final page. Use a run-on hook. A page turn is a natural time for readers to ask themselves whether they want to continue or not. If you end on a full stop you have just given them an instruction you didn't mean to. You have told them to stop. By breaking mid-sentence, and mid-paragraph, you send out a completely different signal: you haven't finished what you were saying so the natural inclination is to turn to the next page.

You can spice up the run-on hook. For example...

   ". . . by this time next week. So send or fax your completed application today and you could win

   Please turn the page..."

The reader is over the page without a thought of quitting – they want to know what they could win!

thirty-six

What about jargon and techno-speak?

Generally, my advice is to avoid jargon and technological words wherever possible. They impede the flow of your copy and they generally make things more difficult to absorb. If however you are writing to people such as hobbyists and enthusiasts or engineers or specialists, then you can use them sparingly to create rapport – a bond – between you and your reader.

Business or home? What's the difference?

Perhaps the most important thing to remember is that businesses don't deal with businesses. Your readers will be human beings first, business people second. There are some obvious vocabulary differences – at home I have a wallet, in business a budget. However the simple analogy I have always used is that I wear jeans at home but I go to work in a suit. Metaphorically, therefore, your copy for a business letter should "wear a suit". You should still write to one person, you should still use a conversational style, but you should also remember the reader's environment and use an appropriate tone of voice and copy style to suit that environment.

Asking for what you want

You would be amazed how many people actually skate around asking the reader to do what they actually want. They seem to want to write anything rather than come out with it! Again this demonstrates lack of confidence. For example, nine times out of ten, if you receive a letter from a charity, you know they want either money or some other kind of support. My experience has always been that you might as well come straight to the point and then concentrate on giving the reader plenty of good reasons to go ahead and respond the way you want.

    This applies to all manner of letter, from sales through to legal, etc. There is no reason, for example, why a letter cannot start in the first paragraph with "Send back or fax the enclosed order slip today and . . ." – then you start giving them reasons. The reader is abundantly clear about what you want them to do and will then decide whether they want to.

Etc, etc, etc.

The use of the abbreviation "etc." is fine in books like this but usually not such a good idea in winning sales letters. It either suggests that you have left something out or that there is something you don't want to put in. Or that you can't be bothered to or it is bad news!

> **TIPS**
>
> It's a well-worn copywriter's technique to picture in your head, as you write, the reader as you perceive them to be. Imagine the conversation you might have if you were with them face-to-face and then write it down. This can provide you with some great and natural copy which automatically arrives on the sheet in the right tone of voice and style!

What's the question?

One of the best ways to keep the interest of a reader is to work out what questions they would want to ask you and then set about answering them. To help with this you might think about the most common questions you are asked. The regularity with which the question is asked is more important than whether it seems to be a big issue or not. If people ask regularly then it is a big issue to them.

> **EXAMPLE**
>
> To use answers to questions in your letter write something like this:
>
> "There are two questions which nearly everyone asks and I'll tell you the answers now. First, . . ."

When you have finished a draft, show what you have written to someone else. Let them read it and then ask whether they have any questions. You'll be amazed how often they pick up

RULES, TIPS AND HINTS

something so obvious you could kick yourself for leaving it out. Or they point out something you would just never have thought about! Be specific and avoid those notorious "than what" comparisons. For example, "lasts longer" (than what?), "works harder" (than what?). Spell it out.

Have you answered all the reader's questions?

Always endeavour to answer all the questions a reader might have. Here's a checklist of some of the things that go through people's minds when opening their mail:

1. When they are handling the envelope or flicking through the post:
   ❑ Is this one for me?
   ❑ Who's it from (you may choose to answer this one later if you would rather they didn't know until they are inside the envelope)?

2. Existing Customers will also wonder:
   ❑ What's it all about today?
   ❑ Am I interested in this?

3. Prospects will be curious about:
   ❑ What's in this envelope?
   ❑ More important, what's in it for me?

4. When they reach your letter the reader will wonder:
   ❑ Why are they writing to me?
   ❑ What's so interesting about this?
   ❑ Who signed this letter – who is it coming from?
   ❑ Shall I go on reading?
   ❑ Do I need this?
   ❑ Again, what's in it for me?
   ❑ Can they prove what they claim – where's the evidence?

5. These thoughts may also cross their minds:
   ❑ How did I get along without this up to now (you hope!!)?
   ❑ Why will this make things better?
   ❑ Who says so?
   ❑ Is it exactly what I need?
   ❑ Should I react?
   ❑ Is this urgent?
   ❑ Do I have to make any decisions?
   ❑ How much is it?
   ❑ How do I reply/order/get one?
   ❑ What happens next?

A fountain of money!

Use "word pictures" in your copy and that will strike the imagination of readers and give increased power to your letters. For example, just this week I had a letter which described a savings plan as "a fountain of money placing hard cash in your hands each and every month". A "fountain of money" is a lovely visual concept and with so much more appeal than "regular monthly payments"!

Keep things simple

Simple language, simple construction, simple proposition. It's so much easier to read and take in. Especially in comparison with much longer and, from a constructional aspect, markedly more complex style of sentences that barely give the unfortunate individual trying to cope with them a chance to breathe and which become, therefore, asphyxiating in more ways than one. See what I mean!

Avoid abstract or needlessly complex words and descriptions. Do you really mean seating arrangements – or chairs?

> **No life sentences!**
>
> The easiest sentences to understand are just eight words long. By 32 words, you've lost them completely. I make a rule of a maximum of 20 words per sentence unless there is a very good reason. Another writer I know restricts himself rigidly to a maximum of 12 words a sentence.

The long and the short of it

How long does it take to make a sale? Let's suppose your letter takes two or three minutes to read – add another two or three for anything else that's enclosed with it and we come to say four to six minutes. So we want just four to six minutes of the reader's time and attention. We can make it enjoyable time, BUT it is their time. Their time to do what they want with and we have to earn it. To an advertising person five to six minutes is an immense amount of time to have to hold people's attention. That's why everyone will tell you writing winning sales letters is not like general advertising copy – and probably why general advertising copywriters don't really appreciate the difference!

But how much time is four to six minutes compared with a sales person's typical time in front of Customers or Prospects? How does it measure up? Nothing like enough. Imagine if a company were to ban all its sales people from making sales visits of longer than four to six minutes. They would be out of business in a month. Maybe faster. No sales person could achieve in such conditions. But to a letter-writer it is a way of life.

Do you think a two or three page letter is long? If it looks long, it is bad layout. If it feels long, bad writing. If it goes on too long, bad rationale or dull copy. The real perception of length is in the reader's head. And in yours. Most people will give up to four pages a go – if it looks or sounds interesting, if they are interested in what you have to say and what you have to sell. If not, you can't win anyway. They will vote with their rubbish bins. Think positive. Keep your self-esteem high. Stay motivated. This is just like any other form of selling.

Remember, as I explained earlier, you'll lose more readers in the first 50 words than you will in the next 250.

Take your time

Don't worry about the length of what you are writing – certainly with the first draft. It is common to feel a pressure to keep things short and to the point when often a more conversational approach is more human, more natural, more engaging and more readable.

If, later, because it feels a bit rambling or wordy in places, then you can cut back. It is always better to write too much and edit back than to write short and start padding things out. The important thing is to give yourself enough time to say what needs to be said to convince a "maybe" reader that your proposition should be accepted. A niggling and illogical fear of length of letter undermines your confidence.

Five ways to start a letter

As I said at the very beginning, it is sometimes daunting to sit with a blank page or screen in front of you wondering how to start. Where will inspiration come from? What can you do to be different, grab attention, relate to the reader? Here are five ways to start a letter.

1. **Ask a question that demands a positive answer**
   "Would you like to see your Internet costs cut by 10%, 15%, or even 20%?"

2. **Tell the reader why you've written to them**
   "As a Internet subscriber who spends over £25 a month . . ."

3. **Tell the reader why they should read the letter**
   "This letter contains five great new ideas to improve the efficiency of your website. And four of them will involve no cost at all. They're free!"

> **Two simple tests**
>
> Can you beat the snatch test? Give your letter to someone. Ask them to read it. Count five seconds. Snatch it back. If they can't tell you what it's about, you've failed!
>   Your letter should be easy to read – check it by reading it out loud. Or give it to someone else to read aloud. Where either of you stumble or have difficulty, chances are your reader will as well. Smooth out any stumbling points.

4. **Tell them something flattering about themselves**
   "As one of our privilege cardholders, I know just how much pride you will take in running an efficient, technologically up-to-the-minute Internet service. Now . . ."

5. **Hit them with a mind-bending headline or proposition**
   "You can own software costing $1 billion for £29.50 a month. And accept the first THREE MONTHS FREE. Yes, it cost us $1 billion dollars to develop, but it's yours for less than £30 a month . . ."

RULES, TIPS AND HINTS

1. Don't assume that readers will read your letter, or that they will read all of it, nor even that they will read it in the order you wrote it!
2. People read letters in three goes – they glance, they scan, and they read. Get each stage right to keep them reading. Glancing is a short process – just two seconds with an A4 sheet! If they like what they see, they will scan. Again, if they like what they see, they will start on the main text.
3. The heaviest readership zones of letters are: the recipients name and address block; your name and address; the signature; the name and title of the signatory; the PS; and the headline. Add to these by using indented paragraphs, underlining, capitals, bold, and other devices used for emphasis.
4. Natural eye directions should be built on, not contradicted. With an A4 sheet the eye will enter top left and leave bottom right. With an A3 spread they will enter top right and exit bottom right. You have to pull people to the left-hand page.
5. Generally, avoid jargon and techno-speak words unless you are writing to people such as hobbyists and enthusiasts or engineers or specialists, then use them sparingly to create rapport – a bond – between you and your reader.
6. If you are writing to someone in a business then your copy should "wear a suit" – it helps to achieve the right tone of voice and copy style if you imagine a typical reader as you write.
7. Answering readers' questions is a great way to ensure you are interesting. To help with this think about the most common questions asked.
8. Keep things simple – simple construction, simple words, simple sentences, a simple proposition. The easiest sentences to understand are eight words long. Work to a maximum of 20 words per sentence unless there is a very good reason not to.
9. Don't worry about the length of what you are writing – worry only that it does its job effectively. It is far better to write long and edit back than it is to do it the other way round!

LOOKING AT LAYOUT

— Chapter 4

Coming up in this chapter

> *Shaping up for readership*
> *Using the keyboard*
> *Thank you, Mr Johnson*
> *Using letterheads*
> *Using design*

Shaping up for readership

You may want to keep your letter looking traditional – and that's fine. But on occasions you can vary paragraph widths to create shape and to make the letter more interesting to the eye. If you take a look at some of the mailings you receive – particularly those from seasoned mailers – you'll get some idea of what I mean. I have always used three paragraph widths, which I have imaginatively dubbed "full-width" (160 mm), "medium-width" (120 mm) and "full-indent" (90 mm). These are for A4 paper. Use them in a centred format, that's to say they should sit on the page with margins of the same width either side. Minimum left and right margins should be 25mm. Generally the more tidied up or justified copy looks the more boring, solid and heavy the impression it gives.

With absolute justification!

Paragraphs should be justified left (have a straight edge at the margin on the left side) but ragged right. NEVER justify both sides. NEVER use a type-size or font under 10 point – 12 point is preferable. If you have older readers – for example if you are an optician or hearing aid dealer or any business which writes to high proportions of older age groups – you might like to make 14 point your preferred choice.

---

forty-five

Use serif typefaces – the ones with little tails on them such as Courier or Times New Roman. It is best to stick to one of these two favourites whenever possible since – being so commonly used – everyone is used to them and finds them the easiest to read.

> **STORY**
>
> According to Graeme McCorkell, my good friend and fellow exponent of winning sales letters, apart from the Swiss everybody finds serif typefaces easier to read. Why? Graeme explains that Switzerland is one of the few countries in the world where children's text books are published in sans-serif type. The rest of the world grows up with serif faces so we find them easiest. Just thought I'd share that with you!

Using the keyboard

There are all manner of nice things scattered around your keyboard and in your symbol choices and you can also do some fancy things by using customised bullet points in most word processing packages.

> **EXAMPLE**
>
> You have all sorts of things littered around your keyboard which can be used to make points or emphasise passages of text. For example:
>
> >>>>>>>>>>>We're on the move!>>>>>>>>>>>
>
> and don't let things get you \/
> \/
> \/
> \/
> \/ down!

Thank you, Mr Johnson!

I never met the man the "Johnson Box" was named after – but I've been eternally grateful to him thousands of times. A Johnson Box is used to emphasise headlines when you want to keep the letter to standard typefaces:

LOOKING AT LAYOUT

```
************************
*   One of these       *
*   little devices for  *    or even
*   focusing the eye   *
*   on our words       *
************************
```

```
££££££££££££££
£      SAVE      £
£      MONEY     £
£      TODAY     £
££££££££££££££
```

Other ways to emphasise

You can use CAPS! Or **bold**. Or even **BOLD CAPS**! Or you can use underlining – or you can use all three **TOGETHER**. The important thing is not to go over the top and over emphasise – it just looks brash and cheap. Develop a system of levels of emphasis and stick to it. By using one thing one minute and something else the next you will simply serve to confuse rather than to emphasise.

Whether you print them or put them in manually, little hand written comments in the margin are incredibly eye-catching. Write the word "Amazing!" and circle a feature. It won't be missed. If you know the recipient's name you could even include it: "Important, Roger!".

Does it look like a direct mail letter?

Does it matter? It's very difficult to kid people these days – and why bother? Better to get a good mail letter than to try to fool people. Fooling people is a very unsound sales technique at the best of times. So, if they are not fooled and you don't want to fool them, make it a mailing and be proud of it. On the other hand, if it isn't a mailing, don't make it look like one. Keep it looking special, individual and unique.

— TIPS

One good, one bad!

The good example first. One businesswoman I know doesn't use direct mail but she sends a lot of one-to-one sales letters. She often hand signs them with a fountain pen and then smudges it ever so slightly so that people don't think it is just one of a bulk mailing!

— EXAMPLE

EXAMPLE: Now the bad one – one advertiser recently went to extreme lengths to convince me their mailing was an individual letter just to me, complete with authentic hand signature (of which I am all in favour, by the way). Even the copy was supposed to fool me that I was the only person in the world getting this letter. Then the idiot introduced a competition with a colour TV as the prize. Now who would run a competition just for one person!!

Using letterheads

If you are sending one sales letter or even a few hundred you may wonder why I am raising the subject of letterheads! You won't have, or probably want, a choice. However, if you are mailing and want to print letters or even to have a special printing of your headings for a mailing then it will pay you to think whether you want to use your standard headings. Many mailers prefer to use a letter-foot as opposed to a letterhead. That's to say the address, telephone number, etc. are banished to the bottom of the page rather than cluttering up the top, which is good headline space. If people know your name and recognise your logo use one or both of these at the top to say who the letters from. Why do they need your phone number before they've read what you have to say and therefore before they've decided whether they want to contact you? Beneath the logo or name, hit your readers (metaphorically!) with a scintillating headline.

> *" I am quite happy using direct mail techniques for letter design and layout. I know it increases readership and therefore response. We even use graphics such as illustration and photos from time to time. The only thing I insist on is that it still looks like a letter – you know, it has a salutation and valediction, a signature and a PS. It mustn't ever get to the stage of people being able to confuse it with the leaflet. Letters are the most powerful thing of all you can put in an envelope. You have to be careful not to jeopardise that power. "*
> **– Monty Dare, Managing Director, Keys of Clacton Ltd**

LOOKING AT LAYOUT

Using design

Design plays an important part in increasing readership. Letter layouts should look simple – not cram-packed to the margins. And it is always better to go over the page (if printed) and to a further page (if word processed) than to make the page look too full. If it looks full, it looks long. Even if it is two or more pages but with plenty of white space, it will look more attractive to read.

> If you are using personalised letters with window envelopes to save addressing, beware mooning at your readers! That's to say someone opening the envelope will get your letter's bottom first. Your lovely headline will be relegated to well behind your VAT number! What's the answer? Turn the letter round and address the envelopes. If you are using a response piece (order card, reply card, etc.) it is better to let that carry the address and show through the window. Then you can "Z-fold" your letter and present the top panel complete with your strong opening to readers, most of whom turn an envelope over to open because they know that's where the flap is!

TIPS

If you decide to use photographs or illustrations ALWAYS caption them. Photo captions get very high readership. Make sure, just as with the headline, it includes a benefit for the reader. Also don't defy people's natural letter-reading habits. Graphics may destroy your readership if you are not careful. Our natural desire with an A4 sheet is to enter top left and exit bottom right. Large graphics placed bottom right will dominate the page and pull the reader's attention straight away. Then they'll miss lots of other goodies in their first glance – as explained earlier in the "glance, scan, read" process. And if you want to position a headline alongside your main graphic then position it to the right of the graphic. Elsewhere use graphics gently so as not to disturb the top of the letter as the natural place the eye wants to go as it comes to the page.

An innocently designed letter-style page ignoring eye-path principles

OWN THIS PERSONALISED DIRECT MARKETING LIBRARY FOR JUST £99.95. SAVE OVER £25.00. CLAIM TODAY.

Dear Marketer

BONUS FREE!

EVERY ASPECT OF DIRECT MARKETING EXPERTLY AND COMPREHENSIVELY REVEALED..

★ DIRECT MAIL

★ DATABASE

★ TELEMARKETING

★ OFF-THE-PAGE

★ ELECTRONIC MEDIA

RETURN YOUR BONUS OFFER CLAIM NOW

SAVE £25.00 PLUS!

A layout which follows the eye management concept

WINNING SALES LETTERS

A typical "glance" might follow this easy path for the eye. (But note just how disruptive the salutation might prove to the first glance eye path.)

LOOKING AT LAYOUT

Material matters

The paper weight and quality, the quality of design and print, the typefaces and colours will all contribute to the image you give to people. When they hold your letter they are holding you, your business, your reputation and your brand values. Ask yourself, does your letter look and feel like you? Does it give the impression you want it to? If you haven't written to this person before, remember the old adage – you never get a second chance to make a first impression. The overall look and feel – sophisticated and traditional, bright and chirpy, whatever – it should reflect the sender's characteristics.

1. Use up to three paragraph widths to add shape, interest and emphasis: "full-width" (160 mm), "medium-width" (120 mm) and "full-indent" (90 mm). Use them in a centred format with left and right margins of 25mm. Always end a page and the letter at full width.
2. Paragraphs should be justified left and ragged right. A minimum type-size or font should be 10 point but 12 point is preferable. Use serif typefaces such as Courier or Times New Roman.
3. Explore your keyboard and symbol choices. Customised bullet points are also possible in most word processing packages.
4. A Johnson Box can be used to emphasise headlines when you want to keep the letter to standard typefaces.
5. CAPS, <u>underlining</u>, and **bold** can be used to add emphasis. Use them systematically being careful not to over use them. Printed or manually inserted hand-written comments in the margin are incredibly eye-catching, especially if you know the recipient's name.
6. Don't be worried that your letter looks like a mailing. If it is a mailing, then it is better to be a good one than try to fool people. However, if it is a genuine one-off keep it looking that way.
7. In the right circumstances you can re-design your letterhead to become a letter-foot. This gives more high attention space for headlines and graphics.
8. Letter layouts should look inviting and uncluttered – white space is important.
9. Materials and the look and feel of the letter should be consistent with the image and brand values of your business.

What to Say – And Getting it Read — Chapter 5

Coming up in this chapter

The pull of a proposition
Words with power
When you write
Adding enclosures

The pull of a proposition

I'm not going to spend a great deal of time on propositions. I am simply going to give you a short lecture on the subject. This is VERY important so please note that my tone of voice has changed to that of a mother explaining to her young child how to cross the road on their own for the very time. But a in a deeper voice! Not a bad analogy really since the life of your sales letter is at stake. There are four steps here.

1. Put a great deal of consideration into the construction of a powerful proposition that people will want to accept. No sales letter, I repeat, no sales letter should be without a proposition. The more you can do to relate the proposition to your reader the better. Look again at the example of the motor dealer on page 14. In a mailing try to break the audience down into smaller discrete homogeneous groups and vary the proposition for each group. The ultimate discrete homogeneous group is one!

2. Consider whether you should add further power to your proposition by enhancing it with an offer – as in special offer – that will encourage action and have a clearly established link with either the product or service that you are selling, or the person or people you are selling to. Preferably both. For example, if you are offering a product proposition which saves time, offer something which has a relationship with either time or saving time – such as a watch or clock. If you are offering a money saving proposition, how about offering a money box or purse?

fifty-five

> *The thing with any sales letter is that you want a response. Preferably positive. If you don't give your reader a proposition to say "yes" or "no" to, what have they got to respond to?*
> **– Alec Cooper, Proprietor, Southern Sports Motors (UK) Ltd,**

3. Now develop a clear and explicit rationale for both the proposition and the offer.

EXAMPLE

If I was offering a product or service which saved time, the headline or first sentence would pull the proposition and offer together and say right up front:

Accept this valuable time saving offer today and claim your FREE miniature carriage clock into the bargain

4, Sell it. Sell the proposition harder than the product or service. Sell it in front. Sell it first. Sell it fast. And sell it thoroughly.

STORY!

Never under-estimate the power of a letter

Some three hundred million sales letters written by me have been sent to Customers and prospects of organisations around the world. The most famous, and one of the most effective, was a fundraising letter purporting to come from the English actor, Peter Bowles. As thoroughly charming as you might expect from some of his more famous TV roles, Peter related the stories and background which I then fashioned into a letter. The letter simply told of his first memories of the British voluntary organisation, St John Ambulance. The first time Peter became aware of them was at the Nottingham Goose Fair in the mid 1940s.

Apart from a reply envelope and a donation slip all the mailing consisted of was this simple, un-personalised, four page A5-size letter from Peter Bowles. Amazing, huh? Letters can be extraordinary powerful. All on their own.

As well as raising record amounts of money for St John Ambulance, my letter – seemingly hand-written by Peter but actually, of course, printed – won many awards and, in its year, was selected as the overall best entry Gold Award in the UK Direct Marketing Awards. About a year later, having achieved all that, the Client rang me up and said "I've just had a word with Peter and we'd both like you to bash out another". Bash out?!

WHAT TO SAY – AND GETTING IT READ

Words with power

When you write, try to use the most compelling words you can think of. Use turn-on words – new, you, now, free, save – and so on. Use as few "I", "my", "we", "our" as possible and avoid starting paragraphs with them. Use plenty of "you" and "your". Use action words – "tick", "claim", "send". Use link words and phrases – "and", "but", and "and there's more". And you're allowed to start sentences, even paragraphs, with them these days. You have my written permission!

On your marks, get set

You will soon be ready to sit down with your machine (or a pen!) to write a winning sales letter. Here are five steps to help.

- Analyse your product or service. Do a little research. Talk to a few people. Organise your facts and make sure you have them straight. Remember to look at things from the reader's point of view. Make a checklist all the features and another of all the benefits.
- "Position" your product or service in the reader's mind. What makes it better than your competitors? What do you offer that the others don't? Why are you the perfect solution or choice for your reader? Make choosing you the natural and only desirable outcome.
- Gear your copy to the needs and taste of the reader. What kind of people or business are they?
- Plan your approach (and, if you are still at the stage of using a formula, select one). Devise your proposition and offer. Choose your rationale. Start writing.
- Check your finished letter against another formula – how does it rate? Read it out loud to yourself. Where you stumble so might a reader. Can you simplify something? When you are completely happy pass it to a friend to read and take their feedback.

Here we go again!

The second Peter Bowles letter took over six months to write. Peter and his wife met me on a rugby field on the outskirts of London. It was the All England Schools Under 14s Rugby

Finals and we had decided we might get inspiration from watching the St John Ambulance volunteers at work. Eventually we decided it was a bit mawkish to hang around waiting for some poor child to hurt themselves. At exactly that time the heavens opened – and so did the pubs! We retired to drier, more comfortable surroundings. The three of us just talked about Peter's life and experiences, had a few drinks and a bite to eat – and parted.

No help at all! Or so it felt. Meanwhile the Client rang every week to ask how it was going. The truth was, it wasn't going at all! Since the first letter was still pulling like a train, it wasn't yet critical but the weeks passed and nothing came. Then, one Friday morning, the Client rang in desperation. He had to have my letter by Monday.

Then the miracle happened. I started writing at ten past five that afternoon. By half past it was finished. I simply told the story of being in the park, hoping that nobody hurt themselves and the job St John Ambulance do – not just for children playing rugby, but for all of us so often and in so many places. Personally, I was happy with it but, emotionally, I still preferred the first. The Client loved it. We tested it head to head with its predecessor and it beat it hands down!

Give your brain plenty of time to mull things over. The six months' wait was what I call cooking time. It's usually days not months! When the letter was needed, it came. Sometimes you have to tell your brain enough is enough and lift the result from your subconscious "oven"! The point is to brief yourself. Load it all in. Then leave it in your head to "cook" it for a while. Don't worry if it doesn't come at once – you don't just "bash out" a winning sales letter. Indeed "bashing them out" is probably one of the most common errors.

When you write

When you actually write, it is important not to lose sight of your primary goal: it is to sell your product or service. You have to enthuse, motivate and persuade. Write to sell. When you are trying to generate an enquiry as distinct from selling something, remember that the product or service is only the means to an end – you are actually selling the idea of replying and the product or service are secondary to that proposition.

WHAT TO SAY – AND GETTING IT READ

Avoid empty overstatements and NEVER exaggerate. Too many superlatives like sensational and extraordinary within a brief space destroy credibility. Instead, try to make your readers be the ones muttering "extraordinary" and "brilliant" as they read your copy. But not about the copy – about what you are selling! This is not a literary masterpiece. You are not Shakespeare.

Stay accurate. Don't EVER say things that aren't true or cannot be substantiated. Never distort facts to get a sale. Your sins will always find you out. And it's usually expensive when they do.

Re-enter Lesley

Remember Lesley, the bright young person I took on as an aspiring copywriter whose grammar was awful and who couldn't spell? On her second day I got a bit mischievous. Lesley joined my agency just as the contact at St John Ambulance had called me to write another new fundraising letter. He decided we had "done" Peter Bowles and it was time for something new. "Any ideas?", I probed hopefully. "Not one, John." he replied, "Not one!"

Oh, what?

"Now, Lesley, the nice man at St John Ambulance has asked us to write a new appeal for them. This can be your first job. Give me a shout when you've finished. And I'll check the spelling and grammar!"

Two days later she was back clutching the fruits of her labour. Timidly she placed two pages on my desk and sat down while I read them. I loved it. The Client loved it. We mailed a test head-to-head with my second Peter Bowles missive. She beat me to shame – her letter pulled almost 50 per cent more money than mine.

I said at the very beginning of this book you don't have to be a great writer to write winning sales letters. I learned that from bitter experience!

Be careful with humour

Don't inadvertently cause offence. I know you probably wouldn't mean to offend, but it happens. The easiest way to cause offence is to use humour or expressions that don't mean precisely what you mean. "To die for" is an example which, went sent to someone who is terminally ill or recently bereaved, can take on whole new meanings. There's no denying humour can be powerful – TV advertising uses it extensively the world over. Letters, however, are not TV. They are a one-to-one communication starting with the word "Dear". Think about that.

Letter-writing is like writing poetry in one crucial respect. And probably only one! Every word has to count. So revise and edit your work. Hone it until it is perfect. Hack out dead wood. Become your own harshest critic. Check facts, syntax and spellings – and don't rely on computer spell-checkers. Get yourself a dictionary and a thesaurus. And use them!

Adding enclosures

When you are putting enclosures with your winning sales letters, make sure you mention them in the letter. Most people tend to write letters in isolation and then add appropriate literature to support what they have said. If they mention the enclosures at all it is as a list after "Encls:" at the foot of the letter. When you're putting enclosures in with your letter – do more. Say why you have enclosed them and why the reader should read them. Explain the highlights. This will increase their readership considerably.

> **When the letter is accompanied by other enclosures it is still nearly always the letter which gets read first. People may often glance at the other enclosures before they head for your letter. This is simply the conditioning of time and it works well for you. People expect letters in the post. They know it will explain things to them and if there is any news, anything significant to know, anything important, it'll be in there. So most read it first.**

Letters nearly always look the easiest thing in the envelope to cope with, the least threatening and the least blatantly trying to sell. There is often a comfort factor to a letter which, once the writer has established good news not bad, a reader will find attractive and they enjoy.

WHAT TO SAY – AND GETTING IT READ

The salesperson in an envelope

What is the role of a winning sales letter? Think of it as the sales person in an envelope, only safer. Unlike a human sales person a letter can be ignored, put down or curled up into a ball and thrown on the fire. When readers reject a sales letter they don't feel as if they've offended anyone. They never feel threatened, intimidated or guilty. Going for a sale via a winning sales letter is very cosy for the prospect. The prospect always stays in control. And that contrasts well with telephone and face-to-face. For them a sales letter is passive. It may also be persuasive, but it is totally non-threatening, un-intrusive and un-intimidating. And you are always, silently, alone with the reader.

Use the safety and comfort felt by your reader to hearten you and feed your confidence. But never breach it.

Heard of the famous ad agency SATI & SATI?

It was named after this little wheeze! SATI stands for STEAL, ADAPT, TEST, IMPLEMENT:

- ❑ STEAL: don't hang around waiting for original good ideas to come to you. Good ideas don't have to be original to be good. Steal other people's good ideas.
- ❑ ADAPT: then adapt them to suit your business and your image. When you've done that –
- ❑ TEST: test them out. If they work –
- ❑ IMPLEMENT: get using them!

But where do you find good stuff to steal? Look around you. Hoard sales letters and direct mail. Examine it. See what offers and propositions people are using. See how the letters are structured. Get on your competitors' mailing lists. Get on everyone's mailing list! You'll get a lot of junk but you'll also get a lot of gems. Choose the ones that will work for you and change them to suit your application. Be clear – I am not suggesting plagiarising. I am suggesting a fast track to good ideas and techniques. The adaptation stage is critical.

Get a pen pal

The last thing I have to write on winning sales letters I have already written. It is that practice really does make perfect. But like tennis, there is only so much practice you can do on your own. Why not find someone else who wants to write winning sales letters and learn and grow together? It could be a colleague – or maybe someone outside your business that you know would benefit from developing this powerful and important skill. Get together and share your experiences and ideas. A perfect place for this learning and sharing to happen is via e-mail. It's cheap, easy and convenient.

Yours sincerely...

There's nothing so rewarding as the results you get from winning sales letters. As I have already said if you can sell face-to-face or on the phone, you can sell on paper. And hordes of people who find they have trouble selling face-to-face or over the phone, suddenly find that selling on paper suits them much more. They develop confidence, feel uninhibited and like the fact that they can inspire, motivate and convince with the written word. Give yourself the opportunity to excel.

There is no magic. No mystique. All you need to know you have now read. Get practising! Become letter perfect!

You may have realised, this book is one of a series in which we are covering a combination of the hot topics and old favourites. Already out are books on the topics of direct mail, sales management, building Customer loyalty and motivation and now here are winning sales letters too. Upcoming are marketing a small business, running meetings, key account management and negotiation. And then some more. Keep your eyes out for the topics which interest you. And remember, I welcome your stories, experiences and feedback via e-mail at jfr@jfr.co.uk. My website is at www.x-s.co.uk/members/jfr

Good luck with your winning sales letters – may they be just as successful for you as they should be life-enhancing for your Customers and prospects.

WHAT TO SAY – AND GETTING IT READ

1. No winning sales letter should be without a proposition. Further strengthen it by a special offer. Develop a rationale that will make the reader want to accept your proposition and offer. Then sell them thoroughly and convincingly.
2. Use the most compelling words you can. Use turn-on words – new, you, now, free, save. Use plenty of "you" and "your". Use action words and link words.
3. Look at things from the reader's point of view. Analyse your product or service. Research it. Talk to people. Make sure you have your facts straight. Make a checklist of features and another of benefits.
4. "Position" your product or service in the reader's mind. What makes it better than your competitors? What do you offer that the others don't? Why are you the perfect solution or choice for your reader?
5. Gear your copy to the needs and taste of the reader. What kind of people or businesses are they? Plan your approach. Devise your proposition and offer. Choose your rationale. Then get writing!
6. Your primary goal is to sell your product or service. Enthuse, motivate and persuade. Write to sell.
7. NEVER exaggerate. Avoid too many superlatives too close together. Be accurate. Don't EVER say things that aren't true or cannot be substantiated. Never distort facts to get a sale. Your sins will always find you out.
8. Be specific and avoid "than what" comparisons. Have a beginning, a middle and end. Don't vary from the rationale. Stay to the point. Don't bury great stuff in the main body and lead off or make headlines and subheads from relative trivia. Write so that you can be read easily and, to check, read it out loud. Where you have difficulty, your reader will as well.
9. Don't inadvertently cause offence. Avoid humour or expressions that don't mean precisely what you mean.
10. Make every word count. Revise and edit your work. Hone it until it is perfect. Hack out dead wood. Become your own harshest critic. Check facts, syntax and spellings. Get yourself a dictionary and a thesaurus.
11. Readers have questions – make sure you have thought about them and given answers.
12. When adding enclosures make sure you have explained in the letter to readers why you have sent them and why and how they will benefit from reading them.
13. Think of your letter as a sales person in an envelope. From the reader's point of view this can often be the preferred kind of sales person! Let this knowledge contribute to your confidence and motivation.
14. Remember, practice makes perfect. Have you anyone to practise with?

SANDY
UPPER SCHOOL
LIBRARY